WILLPOWER

BEAST
Included

S. E. McKenzie

ISBN-13: 978-1928069409
ISBN-10: 1928069401

DEDICATION
To everyone who has been left out in the cold

TABLE OF CONTENTS

WILLPOWER

WILLPOWER

I

Wizard Steve
Sat on a stone
He was not alone

He looked to the sky
And he saw the clouds
Moving by

"Rise up from the cave
No need for flight
No need to fight

Always be brave."
Wizard Steve said
To his newborn son Paul.

"What gift does your new life bring?
Listen to your new heart sing;
So fit for survival, derived from a force so primal.

You won't need magic to succeed;
Good luck by chance is natural.
Beware of what cannot be explained;

For this is what you will need to know;

To prevent sorrow,
In your life,
When today flows into tomorrow.

Never let
What you don't know show
To the Sad Man

For he will take you
For a fool.
Treat you like a tool under his rule.

Always stay free.
If you can
Stay true to you.
;
And negativity is contagious;
People will think your positivity
Is outrageous.

So as you are squeezing my finger
Let all your good thoughts linger
For you can go beyond

What mass fate is said to be.

WILLPOWER: Beast Included

When the Sad Man takes control;
He will force you into a role;
His bigotry will sting.

He will lie; saying he knows everything;
And has a direct link to the Creator,
Even though he is nothing more than a hater.

Fear; his greatest social engineer.

He will kick you when you are down,
He will spread viscous rumors
All over town.

He will try to touch you with his steely touch,
He will always be asking for way too much;
For he will always be the Sad Man,

With so little to give.
He will always be the Sad Man
Trying to destroy your will to live.

You will need willpower,
All the time.
You will need willpower

S.E. McKENZIE

To walk away
From this Sad Man
Who will try to steal your day.

He will seek to be awed in their worship.
He finds joy in gossip and other's misfortune.
He invades privacy and talks about doom and gloom,

Without thinking how we could all be
So happy
And free.

You must think higher
For the Sad Man
Will turn you into a fighter.

So beware of this Sad Man
And the nightmare
He brings.

The pull of his negative vibes
Will be like a Dark cloud
Capturing you like a puppet on a string.

WILLPOWER: Beast Included

He will invade your mind
With words unkind.
His pull has force, strong as a magnet.

You are not the culprit,
As he maliciously throws,
False accusations at you

In his double talk.

Walk away from his pull
For it knows no kindness.
Some call this pull evil,

For the harm it can do.
Others will let it through,
For they have no clue,

Who they could be,
If they were free,
From the Sad Man's

Negative Pull.

Not walking away from this Sad Man
Is your first mistake;
For he is a toxic man.

He will spread his dread
So effectively.
He will gossip subjectively.

So you must act selectively.
Hold on to your love protectively;
For Good Luck grows introspectively.

This Sad Man cannot see
What could be.
He creates his black cloud;

It hovers around his head
Through his negative spin.
He will share his dread;

For his hate tries
To control your fate.
Assumes the right to be the boss

WILLPOWER: Beast Included

Without compensation
He will lead you
Into starvation

Then go on vacation.
He will age in rage,
While you build your life

Free from Strife.

Your pain is no concern
To this Sad Man;
From him you will have nothing to learn.

He is drowning in hate
As he seals his fate;
Love would have changed this state.

But he is a Sad Man
For evermore
Slave to his narrow vision

He can only make
A simple decision.
He wants to be popular

He wants you as a follower
So he gossips his day away
For the Facebook crowd.

II
And the years went by;
Paul became a man.
Wizard Steve had taught him all he knew.

Sad Man
Grew old
And was buried in the ground

His name was soon forgotten
To most.
He roamed the earth

As a miserable ghost.
He continued to kick people down,
And no one could see his frown.

He continued to share
His spirit so unfair.
And his toxic vibes

WILLPOWER: Beast Included

Filled the air,
And for eternity and evermore
This Sad Man became an existential bore.

His existence created nothing new
Left nothing of value
Don't let that happen to you.

And this miserable ghost
Hurt himself the most
As his name was soon forgot

The worms that got
Into his resting place
Found that his core was already rot.

For the evil within
This Sad Man's heart
Was actually tearing him apart.

"Stay true to you
So that you may
Treat others the way you would like to be treated too.

Don't waste your time;
For time is life
And time will fly by.

Before you know it; time will be gone.

Rise up to injustice,
Rise up if you can.
You don't need to put others down to be a man."

These words
Lingered
In Paul's ear,

As Paul grew tall,
There was nothing he would fear.
And he would never go back

To the days when he could only crawl.

III
Bitter Ghost
Roamed the Earth
And no one could see him

WILLPOWER: Beast Included

Though they could feel his rage;
Once a Sad Man,
Who gossiped on life's stage.

People would listen,
You know that is true,
But they hoped for a real friend,

Someone like you.

THE END

BEAST

WILLPOWER: Beast Included

BEAST
I

King of the Snow
Ice melting
Away his Life.

Beast
Roars in hunger
Hunger so strong

Changes the balance between
What is right
And what is wrong

The Food Chain unseen
Doesn't even divide
The weak from the strong.

As Life flows in living streams
You will never hear
The Eaten's screams.

The Food Chain
Links all Life.
Soothes Beast's pain.

As Beast strikes out again,
In conditions so harsh,
No Mercy can be shown.

Beast
Can't gentlefy his Might;
He must fight,

Even his own kind,
He will eat,
For he cannot accept defeat,

For he is not the only
King of the Snow..
As ice melts

He has further to go,
To get his dinner.
Life gets harsher,

Beast gets thinner.

Every day Beast must roam;
For it is not enough to call this land his home;
For there are many more Kings of the Snow.

WILLPOWER: Beast Included

Beast's hunger is his Master,
And nothing more.
His Life takes Life and gives Life,

During a pace which just gets faster.

Up and down the Food Chain,
Of demand.
Beast's fate lies under the Invisible Hand.

And his killing is not about waging War;
He is just an omnivore,
And nothing more.

Beast's hunger grows his pain,
Tied to the Food Chain,
Pain that he cannot ignore.

As he roams
From shore to shore
His killing dims his roar;

For Beast is an omnivore and nothing more.

Beast looks back
To prevent an attack
He must stay strong

For all Kings of the Snow
Can smell Fear; as all scavengers know,
When Fear is near.

Beast can't gentlefy his Might
Or he will lose the fight,
For his Life

Is saved by the strength of his roar,
Strength to hunt for Food,
To sooth his hunger,

He can't ignore.

Beast must fight for Life,
For he is an omnivore,
And nothing more.

WILLPOWER: Beast Included

II

Beast's sons are in the den.
Momma Bear
Is there to care.

For new Kings of the Snow
Will one day
Make their way

Or die as they try
To earn their living
In the ice and snow

So unforgiving.
See how the new Kings of the Snow
Play all day;

Their life is a joy,
The snow is a toy;
Though the pain of hunger

Will change their mood;
As they grow hungry for Food.
And the Living Food Chain Pull's again.

Their mood will change,
In this land still strange;
To the new Kings of the Snow

Will try to command
Or die as they try
To make a living

On their land so unforgiving.

III

Momma Bear is aware
As Man arrives
For he is the winner

Of every Battle
When he carries a gun.
Often he kills for fun.

The bullet has done its deed.
Beast's blood runs out
Into a deep red stream.

Beast survives to roar one more time,
Then his life is done,
And the men ride away

WILLPOWER: Beast Included

Into the setting sun.

Momma Bear heard Beast's roar
Until it was no more.
Beast was only an omnivore

And nothing more.
Momma Bear hides her young
As best as she can

For Momma Bear knew
That Beast had been taken down.
This land of snow for him was gone.

Beast's spirit was now lost
In Eternal Rage;
Black void beyond the sun;

Knew what Man had done.

IV
Jed turned his head,
Fell off his sled,
And Joe the driver had no clue.

Jed
Saw Momma Bear's head
Poke out of her den.

Beast had lost the fight
But Momma Bear's
Fight had just begun.

Jed was still on the ground
As Momma Bear
Could not believe her eyes;

A man without a gun,
A man who had killed for fun,
A man who tried to run

Is no more.
Joe could hear Momma Bear roar
As Jed screamed.

Joe turned around
And took aim
And Momma Bear was no more.

Momma Bear was just an omnivore

And nothing more.
Now Man as a rule
Can act like a fool

WILLPOWER: Beast Included

Owns the night and the right

To the land
Is under his command
Man with a gun

Is the fiercest competitor of all.

For Man must win
For the hunt was deer.
The sound of guns and fear

Aggressor that will never belong
As the ice melts
Beast's sons

Run for fun
For they do not know
What had been done.

As the Sun sets
Their hunger grows;
As Man defies Nature's rules.

S.E. McKENZIE

Death rang from Man's gun,

And lingers in Beast's son's ear.
The one who died
Too soon;

Under the moon,
Without a name,
Who is to blame?

Man hunts in a pack,
Owns a lot of stuff,
No need for love.

Man has the power to rule this domain
As Beast's last son
Roams without a name.

THE END

Produced by S.E. McKenzie Productions
First Print Edition April 2015

Enquiries: 1(778)992-2453
Mailing Address:
S. E. McKenzie Productions
168 B 5th St.
Courtenay, BC
V9N 1J4

Email Address:
messidartha@aol.com

http://www.amazon.com/SarahMcKenzie/e/B00H9RWX48/ref=ntt _dp_epwbk_0

www.ingramcontent.com/pod-product-compliance
Lightning Source LLC
Chambersburg PA
CBHW060548030426
42337CB00021B/4496